LinkedIn

Creating a Great Profile as a Member of the Armed Forces

including 9 Bonus Tips to help you succeed

TIM SAVAGE

Lulu
London

First edition 2013

First Published in Great Britain 2013

Copyright © 2013 Tim Savage
ISBN 978-1-291-40449-4

Tim Savage has asserted his right to be identified as the author of this Work in accordance with the Copyright, Designs and Patents Act 1988

Contact the author: tim@timsavageassociates.com

www.timsavageassociates.com

www.yourmostimportantmission.com

All rights reserved. No part of this publication may be reproduced, stored or introduced into a retrieval system, or transmitted in any form or by any means (electronic, mechanical, photocopying, and recording of otherwise) without the prior permission of the publisher.

This book is sold/distributed subject to the condition that it shall not, by way of trade or otherwise be lent, resold, hired out or otherwise circulated without the publisher's prior consent in any form of binding or cover that that in which it is published and without a similar condition including this condition being imposed on the subsequent purchaser.

*For Tracey, who urged me to write this book and
who is my real inspiration.
May it be the first of many! Thank you darling xx*

Contents

So why should I read this? .... - 1 -
Will LinkedIn help me get a job? .... - 3 -
6 Simple Steps to Creating a Credible Profile .... - 6 -
    Step 1 – Your Photo .... - 6 -
    Step 2 – Your Headline .... - 9 -
    Step 3 – Your Summary .... - 14 -
    Step 4 – Your Experience .... - 16 -
    Step 5 – Your Skills and Expertise .... - 18 -
    Step 6 – Recommendations .... - 19 -
How do I explain all my military experience? .... - 21 -
What should I avoid putting in my profile? .... - 24 -
What are groups and which ones should I join? .... - 26 -
What about my lack of qualifications? .... - 28 -
How do I market myself out there without appearing desperate? .. - 30 -
And finally .... - 32 -
About the Author: Tim Savage .... - 33 -
What people say about Tim… .... - 34 -

So why should I read this?

This book is specifically written for members of the Armed Forces who are currently still serving or, who have recently left the Armed Forces and are embarking on their most important mission yet – to build a successful second career

Most of the advice, however, applies equally to anyone!

Whether you like it or not, every single person serving in the Armed Forces will leave one day – whether that's after four, ten or thirty five years' service. All too often, the most important mission of your life is ignored, forgotten about and pushed away to the back of your mind. Maybe this is because of fear, a lack of confidence or a belief that no-one else will understand you like your military colleagues and friends.

That 'most important mission', of course, is to find and develop a successful second and possibly third career when you leave the Armed Forces. Unless you are lucky enough to be in a position to retire when you leave the Armed Forces, most of us have to find another career and it's a task that needs long term planning and careful thought. It's not something to suddenly start worrying about in your last six months of service.

It is all a bit scary and for many of you, the Services are all you have known in your lives. They have provided a job, a career, training, education, friendships for life, camaraderie in times of crisis, travel opportunities, self-development openings and a huge climb up the ladder of life from wherever you came.

One of the tools you should be using **now,** to help you prepare the way for your second career, is LinkedIn – the most powerful and widely used social media platform for business people.

Let me show you how to create your profile on LinkedIn, what to say, how to say it and just as importantly, what not to say.

My key message though – **START NOW.** It's a tool you should be using throughout your career in the right way.

I hope the following pages help you with your most important mission yet – building a successful second career.

Tim Savage

Will LinkedIn help me get a job?

The most common question I am asked by many Servicemen and women is 'how will LinkedIn help me get a job?' The answer to that question is that, in itself, LinkedIn won't magically find you the right job when you leave the Armed Forces, but it can help greatly.

It is able to 'showcase' you online in a manner that is professional, credible and realistic. It should definitely form part of your 'armoury' of tools to help you with your most important mission yet – to develop a successful second career when you are ready to leave the Armed Forces.

The key to making LinkedIn work for you is to understand how it works, what you must have on your profile, what you must avoid and how to use the tools available on LinkedIn to help you.

LinkedIn is the most popular social media platform used by people and businesses to connect with each other for **business purposes.** That is, for example, looking for a new job or looking for new partners to meet or make business opportunities and joint ventures.

LinkedIn is generally not a place for social chit chat, like Facebook, although there is a place for online chatting on LinkedIn through the 'Groups' section. You can also message people directly much as you can do on Facebook.

LinkedIn is generally perceived as being a platform that is for the more 'serious' side of social media although that doesn't mean you have to be serious all the time!

You can, and should, allow your personality to come through on your LinkedIn profile and in your dealings with people you are connected to on LinkedIn.

A word of warning though – and this applies to everything you say and do on the internet – once it's out there, it's out there forever, so if you wouldn't say something to somebody's face – it's probably not something that you should be posting on LinkedIn or any other social media site for that matter.

Ninja Tip Number 1 – Don't leave it to the last minute to create your LinkedIn profile

Like life's other certainties - death and taxes, I guarantee that you will all leave the Services at some point, so don't waste those great connections and links with people with whom you have worked and get connected now with people you meet throughout your Service career.

LinkedIn offers you an enormous opportunity to start preparing for your second career by building up a network of people who know you. As you should be planning to continue writing to these people, they should be the sort of people who are willing and able to help you find that perfect job when you decide to leave.

The majority of military personnel don't start to create their LinkedIn profiles until they have decided to leave the Armed Forces. At best, you might have created a skeleton profile years before you leave, which doesn't yet offer enough to the reader.

At worst, you suddenly 'appear' on LinkedIn in the weeks leading up to leaving the Armed Forces and you appear 'spammy' as you desperately try to connect with everyone you can remember in your life over a very short period. Why not start using this properly **NOW** instead of waiting until you are months from leaving?

And for those of you who think you're ok because you've already created your LinkedIn profile and made a few connections, you're not off the hook yet, either. Most military profiles are simply appalling and not worth reading.

Now there will be some of you who can't talk too much about what you have done during your career in the Armed Forces. But for most people, there is no risk or security risk to showcasing your talent in the right way on LinkedIn.

All it takes is a little effort, along with my super-helpful Ninja Tips to guide and support you to create a credible, honest profile that you can maintain and build throughout your career.

Try and get over the rank thing **NOW** on LinkedIn and don't be afraid to ask to connect with people who are senior or junior to you. It doesn't matter what your rank is now, you will all be a Mr, Mrs or Ms one day and, for the most part, no-one outside will really care what rank you were – many won't understand it anyway. Additionally, that Air Marshall, junior officer or soldier, with whom you connect, may well be someone who can offer you a job in the future!

Of course, you can choose to ignore anyone trying to link with you and similarly, they can choose to ignore you, but if you know someone well enough, most people are happy to connect and stay in touch. Don't feel pushed into accepting every invitation to connect. You should only connect with people you know or you have met before but we'll talk a little more about that later.

Think of LinkedIn as your permanent online CV - the place where you market yourself to others where you should always want to put your best foot forward. As with any successful business you need to identify your target market and work out what you want to say to it, to showcase yourself at your best. Only then can you start to broadcast out there with a well-written positive LinkedIn profile explaining what experience you have, what success you've achieved, what you offer and what you are looking for.

6 Simple Steps to Creating a Credible Profile

Step 1 – Your Photo

Ninja Tip Number 2 – Use a professionally taken photo on LinkedIn

Here's the thing – LinkedIn is where you are marketing yourself - it's where you want to look your best...or at least not look your worst!

Like anyone selling anything, people like to see what they are buying and LinkedIn is no exception. I see too many profiles of Armed Forces personnel that don't have a photo at all or if they do have a photo it is one of them in uniform or in what can only be described as casual order.

In your case, you are the 'product' you are trying to sell so having a photograph that generates interest in you is a good start to getting the most from LinkedIn.

The photo must be a headshot only, preferably with you looking left slightly or full on so that when you look at it on screen, your photo line follows the page. Don't look right – away from the text that follows. A professional photo might cost you £30-£50 but it will be a good investment.

Some simple rules:

- No uniforms

-
- For men, a smart open necked shirt or best collar/tie - nothing too bright or clashing. For ladies, blouses /jacket – dress to impress but not to stun
- Smile! Mouth open a bit with your eyes saying to the reader 'yes, I think I can trust this person'.
- White background – so many photographers will want to do head shots with a grey background – resist and insist on a white background if possible
- As you are now – not how you were 10 years ago! Remember **WYSIWYG** – What-you-see-is-what-you-get. Authenticity is critical.
- Make sure that before you upload your photo that the file is saved with your name in it, so that Google Images knows who you are. No file naming such as 'Baz looking smart'. I suggest something simple like: 'John Smith LinkedIn'

On the next page are some examples of good and bad photos for your LinkedIn profile. Get this right because many people simply won't connect with anyone who doesn't have a photo on LinkedIn.

It's called "Social Media" for a reason – so be sociable and show people who you are!

Good Photos:

Both facing right as you look at it now and following the reading line so in fact the photo is taken with you looking slightly left!

Could be better:

Nice photos but facing away from the reading line or background wrong

No good at all:

Cropped from another photo | poor backgrounds | Tee shirt or jumper not really the image for LinkedIn

Step 2 – Your Headline

Ninja Tip Number 3 – Lose the qualifications listed after your name (unless it's an award such as an OBE)

LinkedIn uses key words, much as the Google search-engine does, to allow people to search for specific skills, experience and previous roles. Your professional headline is your chance to highlight what you do rather than just use a descriptor such as 'Army Officer' or 'Flying Officer'.

It is one of the key areas of your profile that a LinkedIn search uses to find the right people for others.

The professional headline can contain up to 120 characters so you'd be mad not to make maximum use of this space right at the top of your profile. What is it with all the qualifications that we now see on large numbers of military profiles? Nobody searches for those – ever!

They really don't add anything other than to show everyone looking at you that you are military or ex-military and that you are desperate to show everyone that you are properly qualified in leadership and management or whatever it is you have in letters after your name.

Employers are looking for relevant experience and knowledge, not a bit of paper that says you have passed an exam or have been assessed at 'such and such' a level by an external body.

Sorry folks – I know this going to sound a bit harsh – but you make yourself stand out for all the **WRONG** reasons by parading these qualifications in your LinkedIn headline. I know – I did exactly the same thing when I left the Army!

Truthfully, they make you look just a bit desperate. It's as if you are saying "I know I've been in the Armed Forces for many years but I have learnt something – honestly!"

Now let me be quite clear here – I'm **not** saying that they aren't worth having and that they won't play any part in your future job hunting success - **but your headline on LinkedIn is not the place for them.**

Put them where they should be – in the Education part of your LinkedIn profile.

Anyone serving now or who has served before has a **MASSIVE** bag of skills, knowledge and experience – all of which are relevant and of interest to future commercial employers – note here the term 'commercial employers'.

They are not 'civilian employers' – you are in the minority – not them!

LinkedIn is not about telling your mates what job you are doing now – it's about showcasing your talent and skills to your **NEXT** market when you leave. Personnel boards in the Armed Forces don't look at your LinkedIn profile for promotion and future job identification, so avoid creating your whole profile around your rank and appointments. Remember that your LinkedIn profile is to showcase your talents to your future employers.

I'm not saying you should hide your rank – far from it, but as with all things, there is a time and a place for everything and we'll come to where you should make reference to it later.

I thought it would be helpful to give you some clear guidance and examples on what I hope you will create for yourself after reading this book so here goes.

So let's take a look at a few examples of how **not** to set up your professional headline:

John Smith
Squadron Commander

Jane Smith MCGI FCMI, FAIB BSc, MBA
Capt, Army

James Jones
Submariner

None of the above examples are likely to engender much interest from anyone looking to find you and, even if they come across you by accident, they will hardly make you stand out.

What's a 'Squadron Commander'? What's a Capt? These are military terms that are not fully understood by the vast majority of people on LinkedIn so why would you use them? Most people won't understand what a submariner does, or has to offer, so as a headline grabber, it's not very effective!

So let's take a look again at the same three people's headlines and what they could have said using some key words that will get them found in searches.

Instead of:

John Smith
Squadron Commander

We could say:

John Smith
Innovative Group Leader | Senior Manager | MBA qualified | Logistics Expert | Fast Track Executive | Security Expert

Instead of:

Jane Smith
Capt, Army

We could say:

Jane Smith
Dynamic Team Leader | Team Builder | Degree qualified | Part Qualified Accountant

Instead of:

James Jones
Submariner

We could say:

James Jones
Qualified Electrical Engineer | Team Leader | Delivery Expert | Royal Navy Warrant Officer

Now I'm not saying that you can all re-use what I have created above in your own profiles, but you all have key skills, talents and experience that civilian employees are desperately looking for.

Ninja Tip Number 4 – Use the | character to separate your various skills in your professional headline. It looks neat and makes you stand out

And it's these skills and experience that you should be profiling in your professional headline.

The trouble is that most of you have no idea how good you really are, and how easily your skills transfer across to the commercial market when you leave, so we have to help 'them' understand.
You have to learn to sell yourself – no one else will do it for you and it's a skill you are going to have to master if you want a successful second career.

Don't lie, bend the truth or claim to have done something you haven't done, though, because you will get found out. You are, however, going to have to get used to telling people that you are really good at doing certain things and don't be embarrassed about 'marketing' yourself in this way. It's time to break off the shackles of self-deprecation and brag a little!

Step 3 – Your Summary

The summary part of your LinkedIn profile is where you want to highlight the skills you have that are relevant to a future employer. It's not a place to talk about 'me, me' though.

Think of all the best adverts you have ever seen or read. They talk about what problem **you** have, they seem to tap into what you need doing and they then tell you how **they** are going to solve it. They explain how doing something will make **you** or **someone else** feel great. They tap into people's emotions, needs and wants.

People on LinkedIn are looking for people who can solve **their** problems, fill a gap in **their** skill set or make a difference in **their** company. Think about what skills you have that would be helpful to another company. Talk about 'you and your' in terms of what someone might be looking for, rather than 'I and me'. It's tough because everyone wants to talk about 'me' but you are selling yourself as a solution to **their** problem so talk about it in that manner.

Here's a good example of **how not** to write a summary:

"A wealth of experience in the planning, coordination, management and execution of operational logistics world-wide within multi-disciplinary and multi-national organisations, specifically in road transport, port and maritime, and training related areas. He has provided strategic direction to Governments and major organisations world-wide and has been responsible for detailed logistic planning advice for major UK military contingency operations"

Now write the same thing in a different way:

"Are you looking for a dynamic and proven leader and senior executive with proven skills and practical ability? Someone who can work with people from the Boardroom to the shop floor? Someone who has recent experience of planning and setting up operating bases worldwide?

I'll help you develop your commercially advantageous strategy and then, if necessary, I can deliver that strategy by creating dynamic teams that understand the overall plan and are supported to implement the plan in the best possible way.

If you're looking for someone with great contacts and recent experience of working with senior levels of government and large logistic organisations worldwide, then look no further. If you need someone who can build effective relationships quickly and cope with cultural differences wherever they are working, I offer that expertise.

I'm due to leave the Armed Forces in 2015 but I am always open to offers and conversations about commercial roles where you need someone at a senior level to deliver that next big project.

Call me on 01234 567890 for a chat anytime"

Can you see the difference?

The first summary is all about the individual, what he offers and what he's done. The second summary turns this around into what someone else needs and wants and finishes off with a clear **'call to action'** which says in effect:

'I'm still serving but if you want me, give me a call'.

I haven't changed anything about what experience this person has or brings to the party. All I've done is change the emphasis to be about the person who's looking at you so that they see that you **understand their problems and challenges.**

Step 4 – Your Experience

The experience part of your profile is where you can list all your recent appointments and what you've achieved. They tend to be a bit boring and bland and like the summary section beforehand, most people tend to reproduce their job specification and occasionally highlight something they achieved.

What you are looking to achieve here is a brief summary of your achievements within which are lots of key words that will be found in a search. This is your chance to highlight your key skills and their relevance to future employers. This is the 'meat' on the bones of your profile but you only want to concentrate on the last ten years. Everything else can be summarised quickly at the bottom.

Ninja Tip Number 5 – Create a generic role called 'Army Officer' or 'Royal Navy Warrant Officer' or 'RAF Officer'

This one super ninja tip alone will save you hours of time and effort in trying to connect with people in the future – I'll explain more about this later when I talk about who to connect to and how!

Just like a CV, LinkedIn will create your experience profile in reverse chronological order with your most recent appointments at the top. Try and cover off about ten years' worth of experience and then lump the rest under a generic heading of 'early career experience'. Unless you have done something really amazing fifteen years ago, I would put it all together under an early career summary.

So you could say for example for your early year's summary:

Army Officer (1989 – 2001)
A variety of career development roles including a key leadership role in command of a company of one hundred and twenty personnel on operations in Iraq as well as strategic roles in the Ministry of Defence where I was responsible for developing new training options for 'blah blah blah'. Also completed key stage leadership training courses where I came in the top 10% of students in my year. I was promoted early ahead of the average in recognition of this work.

Now if you are looking for a job in 2013, your experiences and achievements back in the 1990s are not necessarily relevant, but if anyone wants to look at them, they can get a flavour of what you did and ask you more about it if they want to at interview. That's why your experience in the last 10-12 years is so much more important because it is likely to be relevant to the roles you are seeking next.

But here's the thing – LinkedIn is an opportunity to sell you in a completely different way. Instead of regurgitating your profile in reverse chronological order like your CV, why not make it more interesting and talk about your successes in various roles, their relevance to future roles and give pointers as to exactly what you are good at and what you hope to do next.

So why have I created a generic role again? Let's go forward in time when you are trying to connect with people from the past who have also served in the Armed Forces. You find someone you know and you want to connect with them. The trouble is that unless you know their email address (you may have lost touch) or you have worked with them somewhere else, you will not be able to pick a role that he or she would recognise you from. The only way of connecting then is to know their email address.

However, if you've created a generic role of 'Army Officer' or 'RAF Warrant Officer' you can use this role to ask to connect with someone with whom you served. In turn, they are more likely to remember you too and connect back. In simple terms it allows you to link with former colleagues more easily.

Step 5 - Your Skills and Expertise

This section of your profile is a relatively new development for LinkedIn. It is proving popular and is much easier to use quickly instead of going down to the more formal 'Recommendations' route. The trick here is to create the skills and expertise you want to be endorsed for, rather than letting others create skills you may not want to showcase. That way, when others are given the opportunity to endorse you, they will be asked to endorse the skills you want showcased. I'm not going to tell you what skills you should put up there – each of you has individual skills and expertise but I would recommend that they match the skills you want found in searches and which correspond to other sections of your LinkedIn profile. Sounds obvious but you'd be surprised how many people put in skills and expertise for which they have no track record of success!

For example, if you left the Armed Forces as a Private soldier or a RAF Craftsman you are unlikely to have filled roles with management responsibilities so people endorsing you for management skills is unlikely to happen. But they may be likely to endorse you for driving or guarding or security.

You can't ask for endorsements through LinkedIn but you can ask your friends and colleagues to endorse you for specific skills. As with most things in life, the more you give, you more you get back in return so when you get the chance to endorse people yourself, take a moment to do so – as long as the skills you are endorsing are for real. You'll find that others will then return the compliment.

Ninja Tip Number 6 – Think hard about what you want someone to say about you in a recommendation and ask them to be specific if possible. Even go as far as to draft it for them and send it to them for approval and placing on your profile.

Step 6 – Recommendations

LinkedIn recently changed the way that recommendations are shown on your profile. It now places your recommendations against each of your roles in the 'Experience' section for which you were recommended and then shows 2 of them with that role. It also shows how many others you have for that role but unfortunately you cannot choose which ones LinkedIn shows.

The good news is that all your recommendations are still all shown in your profile further down. However, unlike some sections which you can drag and drop to move up and down your profile depending on how you want to set your profile out, the recommendations section is fixed and cannot be moved.

The key issue about recommendations is that you want to ask for as many as possible. The more you have on your profile, the more likely people are to 'buy' you or 'buy into you' particularly if they are well written, appropriate and interesting.

Don't be afraid to ask for a recommendation from someone you have worked with or worked for. They make up a really important element of your work history and this is an important section of your overall profile.

A recommendation, if well written, will explain your skills, what value you brought to that role and your successes. Here's a great example of a well written recommendation:

"I really valued xxxx's support. He is able to integrate himself with the team very quickly, understand the challenge and the required outcome and create a straightforward solution. But that is not all, unlike most consultants he can 'get amongst it' and lead an efficient implementation. He is completely versatile and not precious about being diverted temporarily onto alternative tasks - an asset on any senior management team. He saved my company around £250k this year alone."

It explains what that person did, how they added value and recommended them for specific further roles. Now look at a less well written recommendation:

"XXX was a pleasure to work with. I thoroughly recommend him for future roles."

Now let's be clear here – the person writing like this is genuinely trying to be helpful but they are missing the point of a recommendation. What did they do? What value did they bring to the role? What success did they have? What future roles?

That's why if you get a recommendation like the second one, you should politely go back and ask them to amend it. Make their life easy by offering a draft so they can simply cut and paste into LinkedIn and finish the job quickly. We're all busy people these days and if you can make it easier to get someone to give you a LinkedIn recommendation – do so.

Now for those of you who are appalled by the thought of having the temerity to draft a recommendation for someone else to place on your profile – ask yourself this question:

"How many people find it easy to even ask for recommendation, let alone draft one that you would be happy to accept?"

Almost everyone will avoid embarrassing you by asking for an outrageous testimonial and I bet that you will probably find yourself making it even better than the one they have drafted for you.
That's in the nature of most people and it's certainly my experience. When I have drafted a recommendation, the person approving it has invariably made it better than it was before uploading it. But what I've done is make their life easier by doing do in the first place.

So go on, be brave and send someone a draft recommendation and see what happens!

How do I explain all my military experience?

It will be pretty obvious from your profile that you may have spent the majority of your working life as a member of the Armed Forces. The good news is that the commercial market recognises the huge amount of training that you have had, the experiences you have gone through, and the qualifications and soft skills that you possess.

Now that's not to say that there remains a view with some people that military personnel are unable to adapt to life outside, that they will be bullies as managers because all they do is shout at people, and that they couldn't possibly work for their company.

Well, as we know from the thousands of personnel who have left the Armed Forces over the years and successfully adapted to life in the commercial world, this is simply not the case. Indeed your qualifications and soft skills are in huge demand. Who would you prefer to employ? A person with little or no work experience, no soft skills in management or leadership or any previous 'on-the-job' training, or an ex-military person with a rounded character (having had most of their rough edges smoothed out). Furthermore, a good work ethic, great at time keeping, flexible, adaptable, willing to 'go the extra mile' to get things done, highly-trained in all sorts of soft skills including managing people, budgets, equipment, buildings, stores and most importantly a great team player. I know who I would employ!

Ninja Tip Number 7 – try and explain your experience in terms that are easy to understand by non-military people. Talk about successes and learning and keep it real

So, let's get back to explaining your military experience on your LinkedIn profile. When you are drafting your experience part of your profile, consider what it is you did if you were working in a commercial environment. For example, if you were a junior officer leading a troop of soldiers, what experience did that give you? What success did you have? Rather than go through the usual comments such as:

"Led a troop of 30 men in a demanding operational environment. Received a Brigade Commander's commendation for work done."

What about saying:

"Led a troop of 30 men in a demanding environment. Learnt how to adapt my leadership style to suit different scenarios and accept advice and criticism from people with more experience than myself. I surprised myself by learning a new language to help me with my role and understood the value of being seen as the role model for behaviour and standards in difficult situations. This role thoroughly prepared me for my next assignment which was to attend a six month course in leadership and management as part of my on-going development within the Army. Received a commendation from my superior officer for showing 'moral courage and skilful leadership in a remote role where it would have been easy to let standards slip'."

That shows what experience you had in that role that is totally relevant to any future role in the commercial world. It is written in a way that a commercial company will understand. It reflects well on you and shows humility as well as expertise and development. No copying now!

The same applies to any role in any rank. Here's another example for you. Let's say you are now a Lieutenant RN and you have just completed an assignment as a Warfare Officer.

Instead of saying:

"2 year assignment as a Warfare officer on HMS Cardiff. Responsible for ship's safety, etc etc"

You could say:

"2 year assignment as a Warfare Officer on HMS Cardiff where I gained experience in leading and managing a diverse team of young men and women in challenging circumstances. I learned to take the lead in assimilating and analysing fast changing situations and then present, advocate and implement appropriate and decisive actions. My experiences stood me in good stead for my future roles in operational direction, fitted me to remain calm and instil confidence in others, even under the most stressing circumstances, and to be actively sought-out as someone who could work through winning solutions. As a result of my performance, I was strongly recommended by my superiors for a future independent command of a warship."

Make it interesting – make it relevant to what you want to do next and try and avoid military clichés. If you end up going for a role that is security related, you can always revert to military speak in your CV when you formally apply or when you are initially chatting to the company about the role and giving them a flavour of your experience and background.

Every level and role in the Armed Forces will have relevance to a commercial employer in terms of the soft skills learned, and used, (so that gives you experience) and the training each one required. No other organisation or company offers as much training to its employees as the Armed Forces. Take the time to think about it and it will come back to you. In fact, why not make a note every course you have taken and how you used the learning. Add the really poignant courses within your LinkedIn profile.

What should I avoid putting in my profile?

In truth, there isn't a whole lot of stuff that you need to *avoid* putting in your profile on a personal level. The key to this is to think whether it is relevant to your future roles. For example, if you were a trained sniper, I'm not sure that this is ever going to help you get a role in the commercial world and such courses are likely to be misunderstood by HR people in the commercial world who can't cope with the thought of someone being a sniper!
Now, you and I know that the skills you will have been taught on your sniper course, and put into practice in a hostile environment, are very relevant to certain roles in the world outside. If you were going for a game-keeping role, or deer stalking role, or some of the more 'exotic' post-military roles in the security world then being sniper-trained may be pertinent.

It is, however, unlikely to be the first thing on an employer's mind when they are looking to fill a commercial role that doesn't need those skills. In terms of soft skills though, you will have learned patience, discipline, working effectively in small teams, and a whole host of other stuff.

I suspect that those of you who are Special Forces trained will not want to publicise this too widely except when it is appropriate to do so. There are enough SF networks out here to talk to, without spreading your experience across LinkedIn except in the most limited terms such as "SF trained and qualified" which will mean enough for those that are looking for it. If in doubt, leave it out.

Ninja Tip Number 8 – avoid using buzzwords that are over-used and turn people off.

In a recent survey of the most over-used buzzwords on LinkedIn, the top 10 were:

Creative	organisational	effective	motivated
extensive	experienced track record		innovative
responsible	analytical	problem solving	

You've got to make your profile stand out from the pack so using the same stuff as everyone else isn't going to work. Instead of using buzzwords like creative, how about pointing out the projects where you were different, unique and compelling. Pointing to concrete examples of your work is much more convincing than just passing out a few buzzwords.

What are groups and which ones should I join?

LinkedIn Groups are a popular way of getting involved with and interacting with people in your industry or sector. More importantly, they allow you to get involved and be seen in groups in industries or sectors that you want to be seen in, particularly if you want a job in that sector. You can be a member of up to fifty groups only.

There are some excellent ex-Service groups that offer advice and guidance from those who have already made the switch. These groups often have jobs posted within them so they are worth looking out for. Some are quite specific in name so *"Sandhurst in the City"* pretty much does what it says on the tin. Its members are generally former Army Officers who now work in the City or who have moved on to other roles. If you were looking for roles, or advice on how to break into future roles, in the City of London, this would be a pretty good group to join. If you were looking for a franchise however, it's not really the place to be!

Most Corps, Regiments and Services have their own groups too, so search for them too. I've not listed these specific groups as there are too many.

Here's a short list of ex-Service UK based Groups and other groups run for the benefit of former military personnel. I make no claim for their usefulness or individual worth – I'm just showing you what's out there. Do your research, talk to others who have gone before you and have a try. If you don't think you are getting anything from the group or you think you want to try others you can always leave the group. Just search on whatever you are looking for and you'll find a group!

British Forces to Business
RMAS Royal Military Academy Sandhurst
The List – the Services Business Network
HM Forces
BFRS Military Business Network
Ex-Military Careers
British Military Alumni
British Military in Finance

British Army Officers
British Military Officers Club
UK Ex Service
Former Royal Navy Officers and Ratings
Royal Navy in Business
Royal Navy Submariners
CRABS (Ex Royal Air Force Networking Group)
Royal Air Force – current and former members
UK Ex Forces Defence Jobs
UK Ex-Service
Forces Recruitment Group
UK Veteran's networking
The Service Leaver's Network

What about my lack of qualifications?

I've already talked earlier about this peculiar military thing of applying for a whole heap of qualifications and post nominal letters immediately prior to leaving the Armed Forces and then displaying them in your professional headline. It looks obvious and it's not the right place to put them.

I left school at sixteen with ten old fashioned 'O' levels and went to work in a bank for three years where I managed to gain one 'A' level at night school before joining the Army at nineteen. I left the Army as a Lieutenant Colonel twenty-six years later with a postgraduate diploma from Manchester Business School having attended the AMAC Course as part of my resettlement training. That was it for me in terms of qualifications.

I applied for and was awarded a Fellowship from the Chartered Management Institute and I became a member of the City and Guilds Institute. I also became a qualified PRINCE2 practitioner during my resettlement time. But at no stage did I ever think that the lack of a Bachelor's degree or Master's degree was going to stop me from getting the job that I wanted. You see, my experience was FAR more interesting and relevant than any number of paper qualifications I could have studied for over the years.

I love the fact that almost every single course and piece of training done these days in the Armed Forces comes with a qualification of some kind. That's great and it's right that you should be retaining these qualifications for the future. However, in applying for a Senior Management or Director Role, my experience, training and personality was far more relevant than a Master's Degree or a degree earned some 25 years earlier.

All I'm saying is don't get hung up on any perceived lack of qualifications you think you may have. If you've managed to study throughout your military career and you now have a Bachelor's or Master's degree – well done you. It will certainly do you no harm and in some sectors it will be very important for you – social care, teaching and such like.

But don't despair if you aren't one of these people. No-one is going to ask you why you haven't studied for a degree in your thirties or forties. Of much more interest and relevance is your recent experience, your personality, your attitude and your ability to market yourself in a way that sells who you are and what you will bring to the company you are applying to join. Have real faith in your ability and don't forget that you have completed some of the very best training on offer anywhere in the world. You have a lot to offer – you just need to believe this yourself.

Ninja Tip Number 9 – use LinkedIn to research people who will be interviewing you, talking to you or who could give you information about the company or the role you are applying for

How do I market myself out there without appearing desperate?

One of the most obvious things you see with military personnel when they start looking for a new career is the link between when they start looking properly and their date of leaving the Armed Forces. Now I know that sounds obvious and I accept that many of you will leave it very late to start looking for all sorts of good reasons.

However, there is nothing to stop you starting your search earlier. It's good to get used to applying for roles, testing your CV and seeing if it is getting any traction. It's also a great idea to go to any interviews if you are called forward – even if you are not sure about wanting the job. The more practice you have at interviews the better. And if you do go for an interview, prepare as properly for it as you would for a role you really want. As those of us who have served say – 'apply the *Seven P's Principle'*, because it will get you into the habit once you need to start for real.

Go there with the attitude that you're going to get that job and prove why you are the best person for that job, and if you do end up getting offered the role, you can then consider it and turn it down if it's not right for you. Or even accept the job but with caveats about when you can start and see what they say.

People only look desperate when they haven't done their homework, haven't prepared properly and haven't got their mind in the right place. You are there to showcase your talent and ability. If you get as far as an interview, you have already passed through a number of major hurdles. The company clearly likes you enough to be bothered to see you and they clearly think you can do the job – the interview is all about whether your CV stands up to scrutiny and whether they like you as a person. Are you going to 'fit in' with their company? So don't come across as desperate for the job. Act normally and remember they have no idea how many other companies are looking at you too? Whether that's none or six, that's your business and if they like you, they will be keen to ensure that they get you ahead of anyone else.

When you start out on the road to a second career, remember that your friends and contacts will be willing to help you if you ask them the right questions. **Never ask for a job from someone you know.** Rather, ask if they know anyone who might be looking for someone with your skills. That means that they can then volunteer the information that they may have a suitable vacancy – if they want to, but it also means that they can comfortably refer you to other people in their network who might be able to help you. No-one minds helping people, what they mind is being forced into a corner with a direct question which is potentially embarrassing to answer. Just because they know you, doesn't mean they want to work with you!

Similarly, on LinkedIn, don't update your headline to 'seeking a new role' or 'looking for a new challenge'. That looks a bit desperate in my opinion. Leave your headline status with what you have already highlighted as being your best attributes. Then use LinkedIn to find people who work in the companies you want to work in. See who is connected to them through your connections. Ask them for an introduction and drop them a nice non-pushy note asking them if they would mind having a chat with you for fifteen minutes about their company and the opportunities within it. Note that you're not asking for a job, just a chance to find out more about the company.

Thousands of people leave the Services every year and the overwhelming majority of them will find employment within six months. The trick is to find the RIGHT job – not just any job and that means that you've got to prepare yourself for some serious thinking about what you want to do and where you want to end up. LinkedIn, used properly, will significantly improve your chances of finding the right job. Good luck!

And finally

If you want to know more about me and what I do, please connect with me on LinkedIn at:

http://www.linkedin.com/in/timsavage2000

You can also follow me on Twitter at:

https://twitter.com/ReallyFlyBiz

You can follow me on Facebook at:

https://www.facebook.com/ReallyFlyBiz

https://www.facebook.com/TimSavageAssociatesLtd

Coming soon – a brand new member-only site for those who want more help and support to prepare for their next career.

Sign up for updates here:

www.yourmostimportantmission.com

About the Author: Tim Savage

Tim served in the British Army for over 26 years and retired from the Army in 2008. He is now a successful business owner and Business Growth Advisor supporting, coaching and mentoring small businesses. His next project is very close to his heart – www.yourmostimportantmission.com will offer additional support to service personnel wanting to prepare for their next career.

Tim joined the Army in 1981 as a soldier and was promoted to Corporal before being selected for a commission in 1986. He was commissioned into the Royal Army Pay Corps in December 1986 having completed his officer training at the Royal Military Academy, Sandhurst. He was promoted to the rank of Lieutenant Colonel in 2000 – one of the youngest ever to be promoted at that age having been a former soldier.

He served all over the world from Germany to Sierra Leone, from Bosnia to Washington DC and also enjoyed a tour in Hong Kong and Brunei serving with the 6th Queen Elizabeth's Own Gurkha Rifles. He left the Army in 2008 to pursue a commercial career and has since set up a number of companies.

In 2011, Tim won a contract to deliver a test and readiness programme for the new national Transport Coordination Centre set up by the Olympic Delivery Authority to provide a national coordination centre for all transport agencies across UK for the 2012 London Olympic Games. This project received major plaudits and Tim's programme was seen as the gold standard for other transport agencies to copy.

He joined the Entrepreneur's Circle in 2011 and became a Business Growth Advisor very shortly afterwards. In 2012 he was runner-up in the national Business Growth Advisor of the Year Awards. He now spends an increasing amount of his time mentoring and coaching small business owners and is an advisor to a number of companies breaking into new markets.

What people say about Tim...

"I really valued Tim's support. He is able to integrate himself with the team very quickly, understand the challenge and the required outcome and create a straight forward solution. But that is not it; unlike most consultants he can get amongst it and lead an efficient implementation. He is completely versatile and not precious about being diverted temporarily onto alternative tasks - an asset on any senior management team."

Adrian Went, MD, Griffon Hoverwork Ltd

"What I love most about Tim is that - he motivates people to do the things, they need to do, to get the results they want. What a great gift to have"

Louis Houghton, Financial Advisor

"I worked with Tim via his Entrepreneur's Circle group, where he is the group leader. Tim's enthusiasm and dedication to his members is amazing, he is always available and is always supportive. The group is excellent for practical support to grow your business, with great members whom all work together to support each other, even if they are in competitive businesses, which I think is great. I have a lot of time for Tim. I think he is a great guy... honest, approachable and would do anything to help you if he thought he could make a difference (often he can). Highly recommended.

Mike Robinson, MD, Generate UK Ltd

"Tim is an absolute joy to work with. His knowledge, help, support and enthusiasm for his work are second to none. He has a clear and genuine desire to help all the businesses he works with as the Business Growth Advisor for the Andover, Newbury and Basingstoke branch of Entrepreneur's Circle. Tim has used his extensive network of contacts to open many doors for me which is resulting in tangible revenue generation. I would recommend Tim to anyone."

Lorraine Ashover, MD, Minerva PCS Ltd

"Tim combines his passion for life with straight forward, brutally honest, and direct business advice. His confidence in my abilities and unwavering support, lead me to develop the strong foundations necessary to pursue my consultancy business. I highly recommend Tim and thoroughly support his business growth network."

Ian Payne, MD, IJT Consulting

"Tim's infectious energy and enthusiasm gives you an incredible boost when tackling the blockers in your business. Thanks to Tim and the Entrepreneur's Circle, I've taken a completely different perspective of my business which has so far helped me to double profit and revenue within just a few months!"

Dan Harrison, MD, WP Doctors Ltd

"Tim has a wealth of experience in marketing and business. He always presents great information and energetically tries to help others with clear direction.

Steve Welsh, MD, SWSM Ltd

Printed in Great Britain
by Amazon.co.uk, Ltd.,
Marston Gate.